At Ease, Soldier! is based on research and clinical experience from working with military members and their families. The term "soldier" refers to service members from all military branches. The following comments were written by members, active and retired, of the United States Uniformed Services:

Army:
"This is a great tool for soldiers and I will recommend it to all members in my unit. It is well-written and concise. The topics and sections prompted me to think about things and issues that I didn't even know affected me --- until I dealt with them. I thoroughly enjoyed going through the book and will go through it several more times to get the full advantage of its effects."

Marine Corps:
"Excellent resource for transition back to civilian life. Easy read that will appeal to younger readers. Quick reference guide opening new doors for those transitioning from combat to home. Good job capturing the 'spirit' of combat in short stories. Could see elements of myself in the stories. Not too technical or scientific."

Navy:
"At Ease, Soldier!" is just what it says...easy to work through. It is an excellent resource for those who have been through combat training or in combat."

Air Force:
"At Ease, Soldier!" is a great tool that should be in everyone's ruck! As a member of the military for 19-years, I served both as an enlisted member and an officer, Joint service and NATO, deploying nine times to various regions. This book provides a straightforward structure to understand some of our military members' concerns. The information is presented in a manner that allows the audience a self-pace, easy to read approach allowing the reader to identify or be aware of some possible challenges."

BOOK REVIEWS

"It was hard to leave it behind, it seems harder to come back. *At Ease, Soldier!: How to Leave the War Downrange and Feel at Home Again* is a guide for soldiers who are struggling with the transition from the battlefield to their everyday lives. Encouraging communication with the spouse, the family, and the friends they return to and more. Drawn from the experiences of other soldiers, Gayle Rozantine advises soldiers in dealing with the conditioning of combat and trying to ease away from it. "At Ease, Soldier!" is a must for those facing difficulty from their military careers and civilian life."

> *---James A. Cox, Editor-in-Chief of "The Midwest Book Review"*

Some books are special because they fill a gap and that is the case of *At Ease, Soldier! How to Leave the War Downrange and Feel at Home Again*. Written by Gayle S. Rozantine, PhD, it addresses the needs and problems of soldiers who have been deployed at least once and maybe more into war zones and are having trouble readjusting to life at home. War presents physical and psychological effects that must be dealt with when the battlefield has been left behind. The warrior has to learn to manage their stress, anger, and deal with sleep problems, among a myriad of comparable problems. The author has over fifteen years of dealing with soldiers and their families and has great admiration for them. If you or someone you know has returned to civilian life or stateside duty and think this book would be helpful, you're right.

> *--- Alan Caruba, Editor of Bookviews.com, Founding Member of The National Book Critics Circle*

IN YOUR WORDS....

Here are comments Soldiers and their spouses have made about *At Ease, Soldier!*:

"This book helped me organize my thoughts and learn from things that happened, good and bad, hopefully to make me a better husband, father, and Soldier."

"A helpful tool for returning Soldiers and also for wives."

"This book educated me and helped prepare me for my husband's return home."

"*At Ease, Soldier!* should be made available as an essential part of the decompression process for all Soldiers returning from war."

"This is a well-thought out, well-written book. The author obviously did research into what it is like to be a real Soldier, inside and out."

"This book is an easily accessible tool that offers solutions to problems that Soldiers may face as a result of the effects of war."

"It is a wonderful guide to help Soldiers and their families understand what happens and why, with great tips on what to do about it."

"This served as a great tool to open up and discuss the deployment with my wife and family. It allowed me to have a deep discussion about my experiences in a way they could also understand."

"What was great was it was more a workbook, so we could write down what was in our minds. It helped us to talk about it more openly."

"I found this book an excellent exercise for those who have been in combat or training for combat."

"It helped me as a wife to get a better understanding of what to expect from my husband as well as what he went through at war."

"It is exceptional, because it hits right to the heart of difficult situations that Soldiers face daily in the time of war and it brings the reader directly to the front line without sugar-coating the reality of the traumatic effects of war."

"*At Ease, Soldier!* is an invaluable tool to use as the Soldier returns to his pre-war self."

"This is a guidebook for self discovery about dealing with all of the experiences and effects of being deployed to a combat zone."

"Reading this book was better than public meetings and allowed closer personal time for my husband and I so we could really understand each other."

"I think that family members can benefit immensely from reading this book, because it brings to light the events that they might not completely understand that their Soldier may have endured."

"*At Ease, Soldier!* opened a dialogue between my brother and me about our combat experiences. We both served in Viet Nam but never talked about it. This book has given us something we've never had before."

"The main goal is accomplished. Get the material to the Soldier, educate them, give them a chance to reflect and the tools to make progress and heal, and allow them to move on with a healthy and productive lifestyle."

"Great book and asset. Wish there was something like it five years ago."

AT EASE, SOLDIER!

Gayle S. Rozantine, Ph.D.

OPTIMAVITA

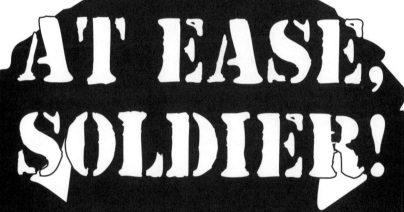

AT EASE, SOLDIER!

How to Leave the War Downrange
and
Feel at Home Again

Gayle S. Rozantine, Ph.D.

At Ease, Soldier! How to Leave the War Downrange and Feel at Home Again

Cover art by Maryellen Courter
Graphic design by Maryellen Courter

Library of Congress Cataloging-in-Publication Data

Rozantine, Gayle S.
    At Ease, Soldier! How to Leave the War Downrange and Feel at Home Again
Gayle S. Rozantine p. cm.
Includes bibliographical references
ISBN   978-0-9797597-7-2 / 0-9797597-7-3
1.Combat-psychological aspects. 2.Post-deployment reintegration. 3. Battlemind debriefing 4. Resiliency training. 5. Stress management. 6. Anger management

All use of quotations is done under the fair use copyright principal. Quotes were obtained from the following websites:
Gen. William Tecumseh Sherman: http://en.wikiquote.org/wiki/William_Tecumseh_Sherman
Gen. H. Norman Schwartzkopf: http://www.achievement.org/autodoc/page/sch0int-3
Jose Narosky: http://en.wikiquote.org/wiki/War

Printed in the United States of America by Malloy Lithographing, Inc., a veteran-owned company.

THANK YOU

This book is dedicated to all the courageous Soldiers who have sacrificed their safety and the comforts of home to preserve my freedom and the freedom of my family. I would also like to thank the members of their families who have endured the hardship of managing the home front while their Soldiers were deployed.

CONTENTS

INTRODUCTION

If you are a Soldier who has been deployed at least once, maybe more --- a Soldier who has been having trouble readjusting to life at home or has a Battle Buddy who is having problems --- this book is for you. In this book, you will find information about the obstacles that most Soldiers face after deployment and effective solutions to help you overcome the challenges.

During post-deployment briefings, you were told that you might have trouble adjusting to home life, but no one told you what kinds of problems to expect or what to do about them. You sat through a lot of meetings, watched a lot of presentations, and were given loads of written materials, most of which ended up in a pile somewhere or in the trash. Now that you've been home for a while, you may have started having some problems but don't know what to do about them.

This book was written for post-deployment Soldiers. As you read, you will recognize that you are facing the same kinds of challenges as other Soldiers who are adjusting to life at home. The information provided in this book will help you identify the areas that are creating trouble for you. The techniques and exercises will teach you important skills and give you tools to use when you are confronted with a problem.

Over the past fifteen years, I have had the privilege of working with hundreds of spouses whose Soldiers have been through multiple deployments. We worked together as they coped with their fears for their Soldier's safety, the challenge of managing the home front, and the loneliness of separation. As couples, many returning Soldiers and their spouses worked with me to adjust to the ups and downs of being together again --- their happiness at reuniting as well as their power struggles.

The work I have done with Soldiers and their families has taught me how your training and deployment experiences are affecting you. I appreciate the sacrifices you and your family have made to ensure freedom for me and my family. I have the highest respect for you and have a strong commitment to assisting you in making a successful transition from the combat zone to the home zone. I want to help you stay in control of the war in your mind and keep your relationships from becoming a battlefield. Writing this book has given me an opportunity to share what I have learned from Soldiers and their families so I can help you with your transition.

In the following pages, I have presented information you will need to help you:

- ⭐ identify challenges most Soldiers face after deployment

- ⭐ recognize the most common problems your military training and deployments have created

- ⭐ develop skills and tools for solving those problems

- ⭐ create the satisfying and happy life you want

It is often helpful to present ideas by using concrete examples. Most Soldiers have learned a lot about vehicles during their military training. In some sections of the book, I use terms that apply to vehicles, such as trucks and humvees, to help you understand the ideas I am presenting.

One way to use this book is like a road map or GPS that provides directions for getting from the war zone to home.

It may help to think of the memories of your deployment experiences as stuff you are carrying around in your truck. You can use the book as a guide to help you figure out what you are carrying around in your truck that you don't need and how you can unload it to make your truck run more efficiently. The book even provides space for you to unload some of the junk that has accumulated in your truck.

During the writing of this book, I shared the manuscripts and materials with Soldiers and their spouses to help them make the adjustment from the combat zone to home. They used the materials, found them to be helpful, and gave me valuable feedback. The book became a joint effort. It includes suggestions from Soldiers and their spouses about what helped them and what they thought would help you to make your transition. They were excited to participate in the creation of a book that would help Soldiers like you. I hope you find this material as helpful as they did. Now, it's your turn!

COLLATERAL DAMAGE:
THE WAR IN YOUR MIND

WAR IS HELL!

"Some of you young men think that war is all glamour and glory, but let me tell you, boys, it is all Hell!"
--General William Tecumseh Sherman

"True courage is being afraid, and going ahead and doing your job."
--General H. Norman Schwarzkopf

"In war, there are no unwounded soldiers."
--José Narosky

While you were deployed, things happened around you and to you that have changed who you are. It is important for you to understand how being downrange is affecting you now that you're home. It is also important for you to learn how to cope with these changes so you can adjust to life at home and create the life you want.

During deployment to war zones, Soldiers experience events which change the way they see themselves, their relationships to others, and their place in the world. When you returned, you were told that you might have trouble readjusting but you weren't told what kinds of problems you might confront or what to do about them.

"COLLATERAL DAMAGE"

The term "collateral damage" refers to unintentional damage that occurs during a military conflict. The war in your mind is collateral damage --- that is, injury that is a consequence of your combat experiences that was not expected or inflicted deliberately.

THE WAR IN YOUR MIND

The most common "collateral damage" that Soldiers experience includes feeling "on edge" all the time, being easily angered, not feeling "at home," and wanting time to adjust to life back home without feeling pressured by family and friends to participate in everything.

Here are some changes you may have noticed and some important questions to ask yourself:

Irritability, Anger

- Do you find yourself snapping at your friends and family?
- Do you go from zero to a fist fight in an instant?

Feeling on Edge

- Is it hard to relax?
- Do you have trouble going to sleep or staying asleep?

Road Rage

- Do you have "road rage" or do you drive fast or aggressively?
- Do you tend to ignore traffic laws?

Shutting Down, Withdrawal

- Do you shut down rather than expressing your feelings?
- Do you "clam up" and "go into a shell" when you feel irritated or things don't go your way?

Controlling

- Do you overreact to small things and find yourself trying to control things that don't really matter?
- Do you feel angry when people move your stuff around?

Locked and Loaded

- Do you feel uncomfortable without your weapon?
- Do you feel on guard and overly vigilant even when you are not in danger?

Emotional Overload

- Do you numb out and detach to keep from expressing your feelings?
- Does it really bother you to see your girlfriend, boyfriend, or spouse crying?

Avoiding Memories

- Are you bothered by your memories of your deployment experiences?
- Do you avoid conversations about your deployment experiences?

Feeling Guilty

- Do you feel guilty about anything that happened to your buddies?
- Do you feel responsible and guilty that you survived when they did not?

Alcohol

- Do you use alcohol to calm down, go to sleep, chill out, or numb your feelings?
- Has alcohol interfered with your relationships at home?

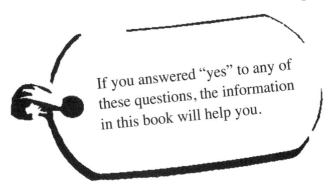

If you answered "yes" to any of these questions, the information in this book will help you.

Can you identify any signs of "collateral damage" in your life since returning home from deployment?

How to Leave the War Downrange
& Feel at Home Again

This book was written specifically for Soldiers like you. Like most Soldiers, you probably don't want to ask for help. It's hard enough to admit to yourself that you are having any problems, much less let anyone else know about them. You think that admitting you are having trouble will make other people think you're weak.

You don't have to be having problems to benefit from this book. Maybe you're not having post-deployment difficulties, but you may recognize them in some of your Buddies. The information in this book will help you understand your friends and will give you tools that you can share with them.

This book will teach you some essential skills, like how to recognize when you're stressed and what to do about it. You'll learn how to leave the war downrange so that you don't have a war raging in your mind. You'll learn how your training and deployment experiences have changed you. You'll learn what it means to feel relaxed again so you can feel comfortable in your own skin. Wouldn't it be great to finally feel at home again?

How this book will help you:

You know what it means to be downrange. It will be important to learn how to leave the war downrange so your relationships don't turn into a battlefield. To do that, it will help if you understand how the things you experienced during your deployment have affected you. You will also need to acquire some new tools to help you make the transition.

HOW TO GET THE MOST OUT OF THIS BOOK

From time to time, I will ask you to stop reading, to think about your experiences—positive, negative, and neutral — and to write about them. You will see that there are lined spaces for writing. If you need more space to write, there are additional pages at the end of the book.

Due to the personal nature of your thoughts, feelings, and memories, it is a good idea for you to keep your book in a private place where others don't have access to it. You may want to share what you have written with family or friends, but that should be your choice. Keeping your book in a private place will ensure that what you write is confidential. If you prefer, you may want to write about your thoughts in a separate notebook or on your computer.

Regardless of where you decide to write, thinking and writing about your experiences will help you get rid of the bad thoughts, feelings, and memories that you are carrying around with you. You will find that writing helps you to leave the war downrange and feel at home again.

To help you get started, take a moment to consider this question:

WHAT WOULD YOU LIKE TO GET OUT OF THIS BOOK?

BEING DOWNRANGE
THE WORLD OF WAR

WHAT IT IS LIKE TO BE DOWNRANGE

Deployment to a combat zone is an intense, life threatening experience that exposes you to the reality of death. As you well know, a combat environment is demanding and harsh. You, like your Battle Buddies, were sometimes overwhelmed by the things you saw, heard, smelled.

During your deployment, you were immersed in the World of War and your reality changed. You were exposed to experiences which changed the way you see the world and your place in it. There is no way to take back those experiences or rewrite your history. However, I will help you use those experiences to make you stronger.

Your training made you physically strong and able to survive. Learning to cope with the memories of your combat experiences can make you even stronger. It can make you more capable of managing crises and solving problems. It can make you a stronger person for yourself and for your family.

Some of your memories may be very disturbing. You may not like to think about some of your deployment experiences. One way to think about the work you will be doing as you use this book is to consider it as cleaning out your truck.

While you were deployed, your experiences, worries, and concerns filled up your truck. Some of the things you brought back with you are valuable, like discipline, loyalty to your Buddies, and the ability to think and act fast and to complete a mission successfully. But you also brought back some junk in your truck, like bad memories, feeling on edge all the time, irritability, and guilt. This book will help you unload your truck so that you don't feel weighed down by the junk.

You can use this as a guidebook but don't feel like you have to read it all at once. In fact, it's better to take breaks along the way, just like you do when you're on a trip. If you drive too hard and don't take breaks, you get really tired and it can mess up the trip. So if you feel uncomfortable while reading or writing in this section, take a break until you feel ready to deal with it. There are some relaxation exercises in Chapter 6 that can help you calm down if you start to feel upset.

Writing about your experiences can help you leave the war down-range and feel at home again. For those of you who don't like to write, that's okay, too. Reading the sections and thinking about un-loading your truck also helps. This book is for you to use any way that you think will help you.

Sights, Sounds, and Smells of War

The sights, sounds, and smells of war are sometimes overwhelm-ing and may have created junk you are carrying around in your truck. Here's space for you to record your thoughts, feelings, and memories. We'll call these your own personal Field Notes. Writ-ing your Field Notes will help you clean out your truck.

Even though you were told to expect some of the things you saw, heard, and smelled while you were deployed, no one could really prepare you for the shock of seeing extreme poverty or being sur-rounded by crumbling buildings and raging infernos.

Field Notes Continued:
When I was deployed, I saw...

Field Notes Continued:
When I was deployed, I saw...

No one could prepare you to see and smell the stench of decaying garbage, open sewage, burnt flesh and hair, feces and stale urine, decaying animals, and wounded or dead enemies or friends. No one prepared you to breathe the foul air caused by industrial fuel, smoke, and heavy chemicals.

Field Notes:
When I was deployed, I smelled...

Although you went through countless military exercises during your training and were well trained to survive in the World of War, no one could truly prepare you to hear the sounds of death. It was hard to get used to the sounds of war — nearby explosions, incoming and outgoing fire, small arms and artillery fire, rockets, mortars, and aircraft overhead.

Field Notes:
When I was deployed, I heard...

Target of Hostility

During your training, you were warned that you would be surrounded by hostile forces. Your training exercises were designed to simulate the conditions you would face downrange. However, no one could tell you what it would really be like to be in harm's way 24/7. When you were deployed, you were confronted with insurgents, illegal militias, native and foreign terrorists, and those who had nowhere else to go. You had to be alert at all times because you were in constant danger.

During your deployment, you were fighting enemies that didn't follow recognized laws of warfare and didn't fight fair. You found yourself in threatening situations where you were unable to respond because of restrictive rules of engagement. Although you were there to help, you found yourself to be the brunt of hostile reactions by the very people you were trying to help.

Field Notes:
When I was deployed, my most dangerous experience was...

Field Notes Continued:
When I was deployed, my most dangerous experience was...

Feelings of Doubt, Confusion, and Anger

Most Soldiers have a lot of negative thoughts while they are deployed. The fight may have seemed pointless, and you may have thought that the sacrifices you were making weren't worth it. You may have thought that there has always been and will always be war there. It may have seemed that no progress was being made, that you weren't making a difference, and that you were wasting your life. It may have seemed like the native people didn't want you there, and you may have thought that they should be fighting the war for themselves.

Field Notes:
When I was deployed, this is what I thought about being there...

Field Notes:
When I was deployed, I felt angry about...

Feeling Worried and Lonely

When they are deployed, most Soldiers miss their life at home. They feel lonely and worry about their families. You may have worried about how your girlfriend, boyfriend, spouse, or family was managing without you. You may have wondered if they were taking care of things like you would want them to.

Field Notes:
When I was deployed, I worried about...

Field Notes:
When I was deployed, I missed...

Feeling Camaraderie, Pride, and Excitement

Successfully completing your missions created feelings of pride and excitement. Surviving day after day with your Battle Buddies built feelings of camaraderie and cohesion. Your life depended on your Buddies, and their lives depended on you. No one but your Buddies understood what you were going through.

Field Notes:
When I was deployed, my most exciting experiences were...

Field Notes:
When I was deployed, my most successful and satisfying
experiences were...

Feeling Exhaustion and Pain

While you were deployed, you may have gone through periods of extreme exhaustion. Weather conditions may have been severe, from sweltering heat to freezing temperatures. You may have experienced pain, nausea, muscle soreness, and other physical discomfort.

Field Notes:
When I was deployed, my most exhausting or painful experience was...

Your Sacrifices

Your deployment experience tested your character and posed moral and ethical challenges. It may have required that you kill your enemy. While you were deployed, you did your job well and made personal sacrifices on a regular basis. Your individual sacrifices have ensured the enduring freedom of all Americans. You have an important story to tell about the part you played in protecting our freedom. It is important for you to know that you have made a significant difference and that your sacrifices and accomplishments are appreciated.

During deployment, most Soldiers feel fear, and their fears increase as combat progresses. If you have been in combat, you probably know someone who was seriously injured or killed, possibly a member of your own team. You may have seen dead or seriously injured Soldiers, or you may have handled or uncovered human remains. Your job may have required that you kill innocent women and children.

Field Notes:
When I was deployed, my most challenging experiences were...

Field Notes Continued:
When I was deployed, my most challenging experiences
were...

Field Notes:
When I was deployed, my most disturbing experience was...

Field Notes:
When I was deployed, my greatest sacrifices were...

"I am different. I have changed."

All Soldiers are different when they return from deployment. Being in a war zone has a mental and emotional impact on *every* Soldier. It often causes you to have uncomfortable emotional and physical symptoms. Some Soldiers engage in risky and irrational behavior and have long-lasting mental problems.

The more intense your exposure to combat has been and the higher the number of firefights, the greater the chance of you having emotional distress. Some of the most common problems you may experience include fatigue, problems sleeping, and muscle aches and pains. You may also experience nausea and stomach problems, a racing heart, shortness of breath, and other physical symptoms of anxiety.

Field Notes:
Since returning from my deployment, I have noticed these changes in my thoughts...

Field Notes Continued:
Since returning from my deployment, I have noticed
these changes in my thoughts...

Field Notes:
Since returning from my deployment, I have noticed
these changes in my feelings...

Field Notes:
Since returning from my deployment, I have noticed
these changes in my behavior...

Field Notes:
Since returning from my deployment, I have noticed these physical changes...

Even though you were surrounded by hostile conditions during your deployment, you learned to adjust to them. In fact, most Soldiers learned to feel "at home" when they were downrange. When you return from a deployment, it's often hard to feel "at home" again. Some Soldiers even say that they slept better when they were downrange than after they return home. You may not even want to feel "at home" if you know you will be deployed again.

Field Notes:
Since returning from my deployment, I have noticed these changes in my ability to feel "at home"...

Field Notes:
When I think about my deployment, I feel...

Field Notes:
When I think about redeploying, I feel...

Here is some space to write about anything you haven't unloaded from your truck that is important to you.

Field Notes:

In this section, you have revisited your deployment experiences. You have thought about the time you spent in the war zone and how it is affecting you. This has given you an opportunity to unload anything you don't want to carry around in your truck. Unloading your truck will help you feel more at ease so you can enjoy your life at home.

In the next section, you will learn how your training has affected you. You will understand how your training revved up your engine so you could be a great Soldier and survive. It will also show you what you need to do to reset the timing on your engine.

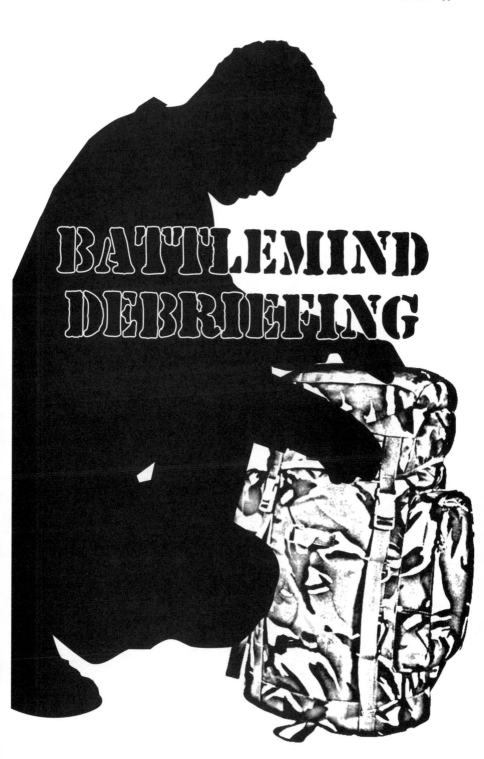

BATTLEMIND DEBRIEFING

What is Battlemind?

During training, you are taught survival skills that make you a good Soldier and have kept you and your Buddies alive. But these skills can cause problems when you return from deployment. Learning about these skills, how they create tension between you and others, and what to do about it will help you to adjust to your life back home.

Battlemind is a term used to refer to the inner strength you developed to face fear and overcome adversity in combat with courage and resilience. Battlemind training, also known as Resiliency Training, was designed to increase your self-confidence and mental strength so that you could take the necessary risks, handle the challenges of combat, overcome obstacles and setbacks, and maintain a positive outlook during hardship and challenge.

Battlemind training includes combat skills and a battle mindset which ensures your survival. The skills you learned that made you a good Soldier and served you so well during your deployment may now cause problems at home. Your Battlemind training may have created a mindset and behaviors which are harmful to your relationships and to your physical health.

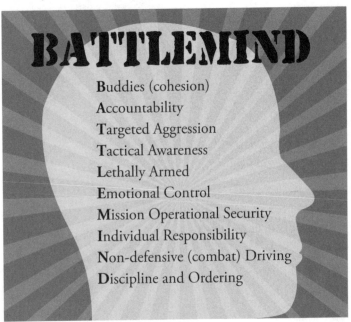

BATTLEMIND

Buddies (cohesion)
Accountability
Targeted Aggression
Tactical Awareness
Lethally Armed
Emotional Control
Mission Operational Security
Individual Responsibility
Non-defensive (combat) Driving
Discipline and Ordering

Your Battlemind Skills

These are the ten Battlemind combat skills you learned that helped you survive. They may be causing problems now for you as you transition from your deployment to home.

Buddies (cohesion) – As Soldiers, you and your Battle Buddies depend on each other to survive. You share the load and watch each other's back.

Accountability – All of your personal items are important. Maintaining control of your gear and your weapons is necessary for survival.

Targeted Aggression – Your anger keeps you alert, awake, and alive. You have to be ready at all times to make split-second decisions in order to survive.

Tactical Awareness – You have to be aware of your surroundings at all times and be ready to react immediately to sudden changes.

Lethally Armed – You must carry your weapon at all times. It's a matter of life or death.

Emotional Control – Controlling your emotions during combat is critical to the success of your missions and quickly becomes second nature.

Mission Operational Security (OPSEC) – You talk about your mission only with those who need to know. During combat, you can only talk about combat experiences with members of your unit.

Individual Responsibility – You are responsible for your own survival, and you do your best to keep your Battle Buddies alive.

Non-defensive (combat) Driving – You have been trained to drive fast and unpredictably, to straddle the middle line, to keep other vehicles at a distance, and to change lanes rapidly to avoid IEDs and VBIEDs.

Discipline and Ordering – Discipline and obeying orders are essential for survival.

Battlemind Debriefing

It is crucial that you not let the survival skills you learned and your combat behaviors and reactions determine how you respond at home. It will be important for you to build on your strengths and to convert your combat skills into home skills. Recognize that success at home is as important as success in combat. You will adjust to home in your own way by becoming aware of what you have to do to transform your Battlemind skills to home skills.

Battlemind Training Troubles

Your Battlemind skills kept you alive when you were deployed to hostile countries. You used them during your deployment and you'll use them again if you redeploy. Each skill is important to you, but these skills may be causing some serious problems for you and your family. Here's how your Battlemind training may have taught you things that are causing trouble for you as you adjust to life at home.

My Own Personal Battlemind Debriefing

When you returned from your deployment, you may have gone through debriefing. Like most Soldiers, you probably attended group meetings and were asked how you were managing your post-deployment adjustment to home life.

For most Soldiers, these attempts at debriefing were not very effective. You were told that you might develop problems, but no one told you what to expect. You had no idea what kinds of problems you might face or how to overcome them.

In the following section, I will provide information about difficulties most Soldiers have when they return from a deployment. This will help you understand how the skills you learned during your Battlemind training may be causing troubles for you now. You may identify with some of the problems but not with others.

Each section will conclude with things you can do to help you solve the problems. Just like your truck, your relationships need a tune-up from time to time, so I have included some Tune-up Tips.

BUDDIES (COHESION)

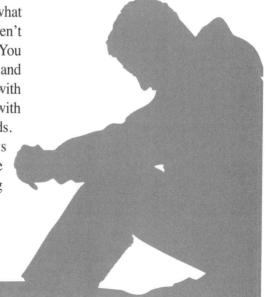

WITHDRAWAL

During your deployment, your life depended on the trust you had in the members of your unit. The closeness you feel to your Battle Buddies is the basis for bonds with them that may last a lifetime. You may assume that only the Buddies who were in combat with you understand you or are interested in what you have to say.

At home, you may think that others don't understand what you have been through and aren't interested in your opinions. You may feel that you don't fit in and may prefer to spend time with your Buddies rather than with your spouse, family, or friends.

Here are some other ways your loyalty to your Battle Buddies may be causing trouble for you:

★ Even though you're glad to be home, a part of you feels like you should still be deployed and feels guilty about being at home. You felt close to your Buddies over there but now you feel alone.

★ While you were deployed, you and your Buddies carried the load together. Now that you're at home, it seems like your family expects too much of you. Sometimes it's hard to be an equal partner when you're used to sharing the load with everyone in your unit.

★ It's hard for you to connect with your loved ones. You put up an internal firewall designed to maintain distance. If you lost any of your Buddies during combat, you may have promised yourself that you wouldn't ever let anyone get close to you again. That way, you won't risk having to go through the emotional pain and suffering of loss.

★ You're unhappy to learn that your friends and family have changed. They learned to take charge and make new friends. You don't want to meet or spend time with their friends. You'd rather stay at home or spend time with your Buddies.

BRIAN'S STORY

Brian has just returned from a year-long deployment. He's been home for about two weeks, and his wife, Tiffany, wants him to take her out Friday night for a long-awaited "date night." Brian wants to spend time with Tiffany but feels really crappy when he's away from his Buddies. Friday afternoon, Brian finds an excuse to spend time with his Buddies and comes home too late to take Tiffany out to dinner and a movie. Tiffany is furious. She bought a new outfit so Brian would be proud to take her out. She thinks Brian doesn't love her any more. She's even beginning to wonder if Brian is cheating with one of the female Soldiers in his unit. Brian and Tiffany spend Friday night arguing instead of having fun.

Has anything like this happened to you? Do you think that the Battlemind skill of cohesion and loyalty to your Battle Buddies is affecting your relationships at home? Are you having trouble in your relationships because of your need to spend time with your Buddies? How is this a problem for you or any of your Buddies?

TUNE-UP TIPS

⭐ Realize that your friends and family changed while you were deployed. Your family will expect you to spend time with them instead of your Buddies. Re-establishing bonds with your family and friends will take time and work.

⭐ Let your loved ones know about your firewall so they will understand why it is hard for you to get close to them again. Make an effort, at your own pace, to allow your loved ones emotional access. Explain to your family that sometimes they will need to give you time and space to reset your firewall settings.

⭐ Consider getting together with your Buddies and their spouses or partners so that everyone can enjoy being together. Enjoying activities together will help all of you with your transition from the combat zone to home.

⭐ Agree to meet your spouse or partner's new friends and spend time with them. Even though you may not feel like you fit in at first, it will help you make the transition from the combat zone to home.

Now it's your turn to think of ways to solve the problems caused by your Battlemind skill of cohesion and loyalty. What do you think you can do to satisfy your need to be with your Buddies as well as spending time with your partner, spouse, or family?

During your deployment, maintaining control of your weapons and gear at all times was necessary for your survival. Being accountable and in control kept you combat-ready.

At home, people may tell you that you have become too controlling. Do you feel out of control inside some of the time --- feeling jittery or having a lot of chatter in your head? If so, then giving up control at home may feel like it places you at risk. You may become angry when someone moves your stuff around. You may find yourself over-reacting to minor events or trying to control things that don't really matter.

ACCOUNTABILITY
CONTROL

Here are some other ways that your Battlemind skill of accountability may have turned into a control problem:

⭐ It is hard for you to let family or friends help make decisions.

⭐ A lot of the time, you feel like you are the only one who cares about doing things the right way.

⭐ You work hard to control every little thing and the people in your life.

⭐ You check on your loved ones' whereabouts, how they spend their time, and who they are with. People tell you that you are being overprotective. You feel misunderstood because all you are trying to do is to protect your loved ones.

⭐ Ordering your family and friends around causes frequent arguments.

CHRIS' STORY

Since returning from his deployment, Chris has to know where his wife, Stephanie, is at all times. He calls her several times a day at work to see what she is doing. He asks her about who she eats lunch with and what she does during her breaks. He calls her when she's on her way home from work. If she arrives home later than he expects, he grills her about where she has been and why she is late. He gets really upset when she spends time with her girlfriend Debra. Chris thinks Stephanie should be home with him. Sometimes he calls Debra to see if Stephanie is with her. He checks the cell phone bill to see who Stephanie is talking to. Chris also looks at all of Stephanie's receipts when she returns from shopping. He wants to know why and how she spends their money. Stephanie has told Chris he is being too controlling. Chris doesn't understand what she means. Stephanie wonders if she will be able to stand being married to Chris if he keeps up his controlling behavior.

Do you ever act like Chris? You may not have realized that your Battlemind skill of maintaining control is affecting your relationships. Do you think controlling behavior is causing trouble in your relationships? If so, how?

TUNE-UP TIPS

★ Understand that personal space and family decisions are best shared. Letting loved ones join in making family decisions brings everyone closer together.

★ Learn "healthy control." In our society, no one has the right to control another person. During your deployment, you risked your life to protect our freedom to make choices. Trying to control your loved ones causes anger and conflict. You may try to control their behavior but you can't control their thoughts and feelings. The best you can do is to try to develop "healthy control," which is control of your own reactions.

★ When you overreact, you need to be willing to apologize. Apologizing is necessary for resolution. It is not a sign of weakness.

Do you think you have been displaying controlling behavior? What do you think you can change to solve the problem?

TARGETED INAPPROPRIATE AGGRESSION

When you were deployed, you needed to use your anger and aggression to make deadly split-second decisions in very confusing and hostile environments. "Combat anger" was required to make appropriate responses to actual threats and to ensure your safety and the safety of your Buddies. It was kill or be killed. Your anger kept you energized, alert, and awake. It helped you to survive. In combat, the enemy is the target. Back home, there are no enemies.

At home, your anger may be excessive and inappropriate. You may feel easily irritated and find yourself snapping at your friends and family. You may feel a lot of anger toward others for no apparent reason and find that you tend to overreact to minor offenses. It may be easy for you to get into a shouting match.

Here are some other ways that your Battlemind skill of targeted aggression may be causing you trouble:

⭐ When you are out in public, civilians' behavior gets on your nerves.

⭐ You get riled up when you hear a person complaining about things that aren't important.

⭐ You feel like you go from zero to a fist fight in an instant.

JOSH'S STORY

Josh used to be laid back and enjoyed going out. If he saw someone in need of assistance, he would offer to help. Since returning from his deployment, he doesn't like to go out much anymore. People really bother him now, so he'd rather stay at home. Last time he went to the store, he got really angry. First, there were just too many friggin' people. Then he couldn't find what he was looking for. When he got to the checkout line, it was long and moving slowly. While he was wondering what was wrong with the person at the checkout register, Josh heard the people behind him complaining about something he thought was stupid. By the time he reached the check out register, he was fuming. One of the items didn't have a price on it so the checker called for a price check. Josh was so angry by that time that he yelled at the checker and told her she was stupid and needed to find another job. Josh stormed out of the store without checking out.

Do you ever feel like Josh? Do you think that your Battlemind skill of targeted aggression is affecting your relationships now that you're home? What kind of troubles are you having in your relationships because of your anger? Do any of your Buddies have an anger problem?

TUNE-UP TIPS

★ Now that you are home, it is important to think before you act. You won't be confronted with the threatening situations you faced in combat. Learning to wait before you respond and to determine if a situation is a real or imagined threat will keep you from snapping at your partner, spouse, kids, Buddies, or strangers. This will prevent you from getting into heated arguments or fights.

★ Learning to walk away from situations when you feel angry will prevent conflict and will keep your relationships from becoming a battlefield.

Now it's your turn to think of ways to solve the problems caused by your Battlemind skill of targeted aggression. What can you do to manage your anger better?

TACTICAL AWARENESS HYPERVIGILANCE

During your deployment, your survival depended on your being alert and aware of your surroundings at all times so you could react immediately to sudden changes like mortar attacks or sniper fire.

At home, you may continue to feel keyed up or revved up all the time, especially when you are in large groups or situations where you feel confined. Consequently, you may avoid being in large groups or in unfamiliar places. You may feel like someone is watching you or you may look for danger when it's not there.

Here are some other ways your Battlemind skill of tactical awareness may be causing hypervigilence and trouble for you at home:

⭐ It's hard for you to relax.

⭐ You're still jumping at loud noises.

⭐ It's hard for you to go to sleep and stay asleep.

⭐ You may be having nightmares.

⭐ You may wake up in the middle of the night and think there's something outside your house.

⭐ When you are sitting down in public, you may not want anyone to sit behind you.

MELANIE'S STORY

Melanie has been at home from her deployment for several months. She's still having a hard time relaxing. She used to like going out to eat and to the movies. Now she doesn't like going out in public because it feels like someone is watching her. She doesn't like going to the movies because she doesn't like anyone sitting behind her. If she does agree to go out to eat with her boyfriend, she has to sit with her back to the wall. Melanie is very jumpy when she drives on the highway. She is especially bothered by dead animals or pieces of tires from truck blow-outs on the side of the road. She knows they are harmless, but they remind her of the constant danger of roadside bombings during her deployment. Melanie ducks when she hears loud noises like slamming car doors. Her hypervigilence prevents her from going out and having a good time.

Does Melanie's story sound familiar? Do you think your Battlemind skill of tactical awareness is affecting you now that you are home? What kind of troubles are you having because of your edginess and discomfort in groups, crowds, and unfamiliar places? How hard is it for you to relax?   Do any of your Buddies have problems relaxing?

TUNE-UP TIPS

★ Recognize that since staying safe during combat required sustained attention and alertness at all times, it will take time to learn to relax now that you are home.

★ Study the section on managing stress in Chapter 6 and spend time every day practicing relaxation techniques.

★ Create a *code word* to use to help you remember to relax. Good code words include *breathe, easy, relax, cool, quiet, peace, still,* and *calm.* The use of the "code word" will remind you to take a deep breath and relax when you need a time out.

★ Be careful not to turn to alcohol to take the edge off, calm you down, or put you to sleep.

What do you think you or your Buddies can do to solve the problems being caused by your Battlemind skill of tactical awareness?

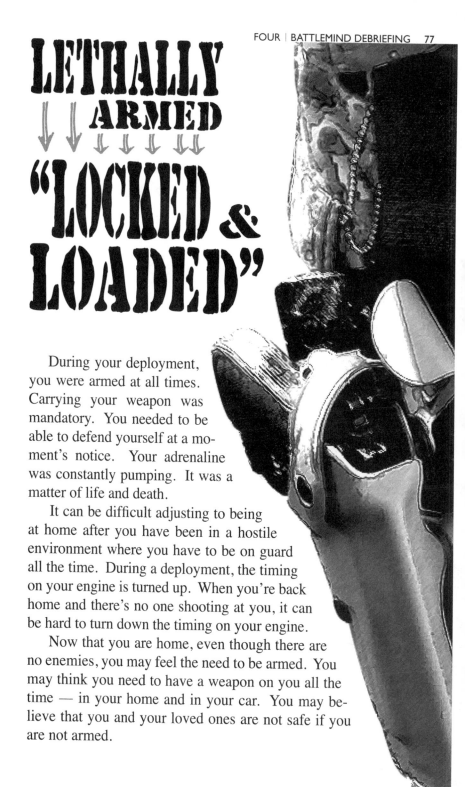

LETHALLY ARMED

"LOCKED & LOADED"

During your deployment, you were armed at all times. Carrying your weapon was mandatory. You needed to be able to defend yourself at a moment's notice. Your adrenaline was constantly pumping. It was a matter of life and death.

It can be difficult adjusting to being at home after you have been in a hostile environment where you have to be on guard all the time. During a deployment, the timing on your engine is turned up. When you're back home and there's no one shooting at you, it can be hard to turn down the timing on your engine.

Now that you are home, even though there are no enemies, you may feel the need to be armed. You may think you need to have a weapon on you all the time — in your home and in your car. You may believe that you and your loved ones are not safe if you are not armed.

Here are some of the ways your Battlemind training for being lethally armed may create trouble for you at home:

⭐ You drive with a loaded weapon.

⭐ You sleep with a loaded weapon next to your bed.

⭐ You have used your weapon to threaten or intimidate someone you love.

MATT'S STORY

Matt served downrange during a twelve-month deployment and was in a number of firefights. He got used to listening for incoming mortars, even when he was asleep. He could never let his guard down, and he saw a lot of death and destruction. Now that he is home, everything seems too quiet. Even though he realizes that he's not surrounded by enemies and that he won't be confronted with the threat that surrounded him during combat, he still doesn't feel safe. He always sleeps with a loaded gun next to his bed. This frightens his wife, Laura, because she's afraid Matt will get up during the night and accidentally shoot someone.

Do you ever feel like Matt? Do you think your Battlemind skill of being lethally armed and combat-ready is affecting you now that you are at home?   What kind of troubles are you having because of your need to feel armed at all times?

TUNE-UP TIPS

★ Realize that carrying a loaded weapon in your car or keeping an unsecured loaded weapon at home is dangerous.

★ Gun laws vary from state to state, but you must follow all laws and safety precautions regarding weapons.

★ Resist the urge to have a weapon "locked and loaded" and never drive with a loaded weapon.

★ Never use a weapon to intimidate or threaten a loved one.

★ If you feel the need for extra protection, you might consider having an alarm system installed in your home.

Now it's your turn to think of ways to solve the problems caused by your Battlemind skill of being armed at all times. What do you think you can do to feel more comfortable without your weapon now that you are home?

_____

_____

_____

_____

_____

_____

_____

_____

_____

_____

EMOTIONAL CONTROL

↓ ↓ ↓ ↓ ↓ ↓ ↓ ↓ ↓

ANGER/DETACHMENT

During your deployment, controlling your emotions was critical for mission success and quickly became second nature. Now that you're at home, you may still keep your thoughts and feelings to yourself. You may have noticed that you are less tolerant, less patient, and more likely to get ticked off. In fact, anger may be the only emotion you can feel.

Here are some other ways your Battlemind skill of emotional control may be causing trouble for you:

⭐ You feel irritated when someone talks about their feelings.

⭐ You think it's weak to admit that you feel sad or anxious.

⭐ You "clam up" and "go into a shell" when you feel irritated or things don't go your way.

⭐ It really bothers you to see your spouse or girlfriend crying. You want her to control her emotions as well as you do.

BRAD'S STORY

Brad was a sniper during combat. Before his deployment, he liked to get together with his friends. After returning home, Brad became quiet and withdrawn. He spent a lot of time in his room lying in bed and looking at the ceiling. When his girlfriend, Jennifer, would come over to visit, she sometimes cried for no real reason. It would make Brad very angry. Sometimes he yelled at her and told her that she didn't have any right to cry. He told her she was acting like a baby and that he wanted her to control her emotions better when she was around him. This made Jennifer cry even more. They had a lot of arguments and broke up several times. Someday, Jennifer wants to marry Brad, but she's worried that Brad will expect her to keep her feelings to herself. She's not sure their relationship will make it. She can't tell Brad because he just won't listen. Brad and Jennifer's relationship is in real trouble.

Has anything like this happened to you and your spouse or girlfriend? Do you think your Battlemind skill of emotional control is affecting your relationships now that you're home? What kind of troubles are you having because you keep your feelings inside?

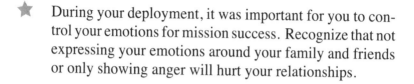

★ During your deployment, it was important for you to control your emotions for mission success. Recognize that not expressing your emotions around your family and friends or only showing anger will hurt your relationships.

★ Understand that expressing your emotions appropriately to your spouse and to your friends is an important part of keeping your personal relationships healthy.

★ Realize that emotional control involves both holding in and expressing emotions and that you are not being weak or unmilitary when you let someone know how you feel.

Now it's your turn to think of ways to solve the problems caused by your Battlemind skill of emotional control. How can you begin to let your friends and family know how you feel? Is there anything they can do to make it easier for you?

_____

_____

_____

_____

_____

_____

_____

_____

_____

_____

MISSION
OPSEC

V V V V V V V

SECRETIVENESS

As you well know, Operations Security, known as OPSEC, protected your operations by preventing potential adversaries from discovering critical information about your missions. Your success depended on secrecy and surprise.

During your deployment, you were not supposed to talk about your mission to anyone except those who needed to know. You had to be secretive to protect yourself and your Buddies. You could only talk about your combat experiences and missions with members of your unit or those who had "been there and done that."

At home, you may still have an "OPSEC mindset." You may feel like you have to keep things to yourself and that you can't let your guard down. Consequently, you may avoid sharing any of your deployment experiences with your loved ones.

Do you find yourself avoiding conversations about your deployment? Do you feel irritated or angry when someone asks you to tell them about what you did during deployment?

Here are some ways your Battlemind training for mission OPSEC may be causing trouble for you now that you're at home:

★ You have a tendency toward being secretive.

★ Questions about what you did during your deployment annoy you.

★ When you are in crowds, you feel like you are being watched.

★ You feel suspicious when people ask you where you are going or what you are going to do.

★ You worry that you will put other Soldiers at risk if you talk about your deployment experiences.

KEN'S STORY

During his deployment, Ken performed a lot of combat missions downrange. It was critically important for him to keep information about the plans and progress of his missions a secret. Now that he is home, he still feels like he has to keep information about his deployment to himself. He feels angry when his friends and family ask him what he did while he was deployed. It seems like everybody wants to know what he did while he was over there. He wonders why they don't they realize that he doesn't want to talk about it. For one thing, Ken has a lot of bad memories that he doesn't want to think about. Thinking and talking about what happened sometimes causes him to have bad dreams. To make matters worse, Ken is afraid that his friends and family might talk about his experiences with other people. He's afraid that might put other Soldiers at risk. When his girlfriend or family want to talk with him about his deployment, Ken often goes into his room and stays there by himself. This makes them feel like he is shutting them out. Other times, Ken gets angry and "goes off" on them. This makes them feel confused. If they don't know what Ken has been through, how are they supposed to understand what's going on with him and help him with his transition?

Are you more secretive since you returned home? Do you think your Battlemind skill of maintaining OPSEC is affecting your relationships? What kind of troubles are you having because of your suspicions and secretiveness?

TUNE-UP TIPS

★ Consider that your family needs to know about some of your deployment experiences so they can better understand you.

★ Realize that you have an important story to tell, because you have performed a heroic and courageous service for your country. Tell your story the way you want to tell it and be proud of your service.

★ Because of your tendency toward secrecy and the "need to know" principle, you may avoid telling your spouse, family, or friends where you are going or when you will be back. You may even feel suspicious when they ask. It will help if you realize that those who "need to know" include your family and friends.

Now it's your turn to think of ways to solve the problems caused by your Battlemind skill of maintaining OPSEC. What do you think you can do to overcome your need for secrecy? What can others do to help you?

_____

_____

_____

_____

_____

_____

_____

_____

INDIVIDUAL
RESPONSIBILITY
GUILT

During your deployment, your responsibility was to survive and to do your best to keep your Battle Buddies alive. In spite of your efforts, some of your Buddies may have been injured or killed. You may have even witnessed their death or injury, which has left you with some bad memories and feelings. Some Soldiers feel relieved that they weren't injured or killed. Others wonder why they were spared when their Buddies weren't.

At home, you may be bothered by your combat memories. Although they don't realize it, for some Soldiers, guilt takes over their lives. They may use alcohol, cigarettes, or drugs to numb out, take away the bad memories and feelings, and ease their guilt.

Are you bothered by some of your combat memories? Do you feel like you failed your Buddies if they were injured or killed? Do you feel responsible and guilty that you survived when they did not?

Here are some other ways your Battlemind skill of individual responsibility may be causing you trouble:

★   Your friends and loved ones tell you that you have changed.

★   You numb out and detach to keep from feeling or expressing your emotions.

★   You tend to smoke or drink more or you take drugs to ease your negative feelings.

STEVE'S STORY

While Steve and his Buddies were searching an enemy vehicle, the driver pulled the pin from a grenade. One of Steve's Buddies named Jim threw himself over the grenade, which prevented the other Soldiers from being killed. Although some of the Soldiers were injured, Jim took the full brunt of the explosion and died from his injuries. Steve remembers the incident vividly and sometimes has nightmares about it. He has thought a lot about what happened and thinks he could have done something to save Jim. Steve's guilty feelings have gotten worse since he returned home. He has been drinking more and smoking weed to try to ease his guilt. One night, Steve crashed his car after drinking with some of his Buddies. His girlfriend, Denise, was seriously injured, and he was charged with a felony. Steve is in a lot of trouble now because he didn't recognize how much his guilt over Jim's death was affecting him.

Has anything happened that made you feel or act like Steve? How do you think your Battlemind skill of being loyal to your Battle Buddies is affecting your relationships here at home? What kind of troubles are you having because of the memories of your deployment?

TUNE-UP TIPS

★ Recognize that you did everything you could do to protect yourself and your Buddies while you were deployed. Understand that there are limits to what a person can do to prevent death and injuries.

★ Don't allow *survivor guilt* to overcome you. Realize that your Buddy would want you to move forward with your life.

★ Notice if you start to have relationship problems or if your friends and loved ones tell you that you have changed.

★ When you notice that something is triggering guilty feelings, don't shut your friends and family out. Tell them what is going on. Remember that you may have put up a firewall to protect you from the pain of further loss. Let them know what's going on and tell them that it's taking you some time to change your firewall settings.

Now it's your turn to think of ways to solve the problems caused by your Battlemind skill of individual responsibility. What do you think you can do to deal with any guilt you may feel about what happened to your Buddies?

NON-DEFENSIVE (COMBAT) AGGRESSIVE DRIVING

During your deployment, you had to drive fast and unpredictably, using rapid lane changes and keeping other vehicles at a distance to protect yourself and your Battle Buddies. Speed and sudden changes were essential to avoid roadside bombs and ambush. The increased speed and freedom felt good, so you didn't mind driving through a combat zone.

Although combat driving may feel right when you are at home, driving your motorcycle, car, truck, or personal SUV the way you drove a Humvee while you were deployed will get you in trouble. Speeding, aggressive driving, and straddling the middle line increases the likelihood that you will get a ticket or be in an accident

Does driving in traffic irritate you? Do you get angry with other drivers because they seem to be driving too slowly? Do you tend to ignore traffic laws? Have you gotten speeding tickets or had accidents since you returned home?

Here are some other ways your Battlemind skill of combat driving may be causing you trouble.

⭐   When you are driving, you feel jittery and on edge.

⭐   You are inclined to have "road rage."

⭐   Friends and family members are afraid to ride with you.

⭐   Since you returned from your deployment, you tend to drive too fast.

JAY'S STORY

Jay got used to driving a Humvee while he was deployed. When he was driving in a hummer, all he had to do was speed up behind a car and honk and they got out of the way immediately. Even when Jay didn't need to, he'd sit on the horn, speed up, tailgate cars, and drive his hummer too fast. It was so much fun to see everybody scramble to get out of the way of him and his hummer. Now that Jay's at home, he wants to drive the same way. Driving is the number one trigger for his anger. One day, after a couple of drinks, he decided to drive his truck down the street like it was a Humvee. He would drive right up on the drivers' back bumpers and honk until they would get out of the way. He went from car to car. The drivers seemed scared and moved over right away. Pretty soon, a cop spotted Jay and he was pulled over and got a DUI. Now he's in trouble with his Commander. Not only will Jay have to pay a fine and attend DUI classes, he will have to report to the Commander on weekend mornings to discourage him from drinking too much the night before.

Has anything like this happened to you? Do you think your Battlemind skill of combat driving is affecting you now that you are at home? What kind of troubles are you or your Buddies having because of aggressive driving?

TUNE-UP TIPS

★ Realize that driving accidents, both in privately owned vehicles and Army motor vehicles, are the number one killer of Soldiers in combat and in civilian life.

★ Remember that you worked hard to survive your combat experiences. Now that you're home, don't risk your life because of aggressive driving.

★ At home, you will have to learn to control your anger and shift from offensive to defensive driving.

★ Be sure to obey traffic laws, use your turn signals, and *slow down*.

Now it's your turn to think of ways to solve the problems caused by your Battlemind skill of defensive driving. What do you think you can do to drive more safely?

_____

_____

_____

_____

_____

_____

_____

_____

_____

_____

_____

DISCIPLINE AND ORDERING CONFLICT

During your deployment, your survival depended on discipline and obeying orders. Following orders protected you and those around you and kept you safe and in control. Giving and following orders required a clear chain of command.

This does not exist within relationships with your family and friends. At home, if you try to order them around, you will cause conflicts and arguments.

Do people tell you that you are being too inflexible or rigid? Do you get into frequent arguments because you have been trying to order your family and friends around?

Here are some other ways your Battlemind training of discipline and ordering may be causing you trouble:

⭐   You feel like you are in a power struggle all the time with your partner or spouse.

⭐   You tend to bark orders at your girlfriend, boyfriend, spouse, or children.

⭐   You are having ongoing conflicts with your partner or spouse over making decisions.

⭐   When you tell people to do something, you expect them to do it. It pisses you off when they say you don't have the right to order them around.

ERIC'S STORY

Eric has been a Soldier for several years and is used to the structure the military provides. He knows exactly what he is expected to do and how to do it. If he has a question, he knows who to ask to get the answer. Being at home sometimes makes Eric uncomfortable. His wife, Sharon, expects to be an "equal partner," which Eric thinks is stupid. Eric wonders why Sharon doesn't recognize that he should be in charge. He thinks Sharon should do what he tells her to do instead of challenging his authority. Eric thinks, "Doesn't she realize she's just a woman? She needs me to tell her what to do." Eric and Sharon argue about everything. They are locked in a power struggle and don't know how to get out of it. Sharon wants to go see the Chaplain. Eric doesn't think it will help.

Have you ever acted or felt like Eric? Do you think your Battlemind skill of being disciplined and obeying orders is affecting your
relationships at home? What kind of troubles are you having because of your rigid behavior?

TUNE-UP TIPS

★ When you find that your relationships aren't going well or if you are in constant conflict about making decisions, consider that you may be acting too rigid.

★ Consider that your family and friends have managed well while you have been away. They may have developed new ways of doing things and will resent your efforts to control them.

★ Remember that your family and friends are not members of your military unit, and always be prepared to negotiate.

Now it's your turn to think of ways to solve the problems caused by your Battlemind skills of discipline and ordering. What do you think you can do to share the responsibility for making decisions with your spouse or partner?

_____

_____

_____

_____

_____

_____

_____

_____

_____

_____

_____

_____

_____

_____

IN COMBAT	AT HOME
Buddies (Cohesion) Your life depended on your trust in the Buddies in your unit. No one really understood what you were going through except your Buddies who were there.	***Withdrawal*** You may feel that others don't understand what you have been through and that you don't fit in. You may prefer to spend time with your Battle Buddies.
Accountability Maintaining control of your weapon and gear at all times was necessary for survival. Being accountable and in control kept you combat-ready.	***Control*** People may tell you that you have become too controlling. You may overreact to minor events or try to control things that don't really matter.
Targeted Aggression You needed to use your anger and aggression to make deadly split-second decisions in confusing and hostile environments. Your anger kept you energized, alert, and awake.	***Inappropriate Aggression*** Your anger may be excessive and inappropriate. You may find that you have a lot of anger toward others for no apparent reason and tend to overreact to minor offenses.
Tactical Awareness Your survival depended on your being alert and aware of your surroundings at all times so you could react immediately to sudden changes.	***Hypervigilance*** You may feel keyed up or revved up all the time, especially when you are in large groups or situations where you feel confined.
Lethally Armed During your deployment, you were armed at all times. Carrying your weapon was mandatory. It was a matter of life and death.	***Locked & Loaded*** You may feel the need to continue to be armed at all times. You may believe that you and your loved ones are not safe if you are not armed.
Emotional Control Controlling your emotions was critical for mission success and quickly became second nature.	***Anger/Detachment*** You keep your thoughts and feelings to yourself. You shut down rather than expressing your feelings.

B
A
T
T
L
E

IN COMBAT	AT HOME
Mission OPSEC You were not supposed to talk about your mission to anyone except those who needed to know. You could only talk about your combat experiences and missions with members of your unit or those who had "been there and done that."	**Secretiveness** You may avoid sharing any of your deployment experiences with loved ones. You may feel angry when someone asks you about your experiences during deployment.
Individual Responsibility Your responsibility was to survive and to do your best to keep your Buddies alive. It was important for you to control your emotions for mission success.	**Guilt** You may be bothered by your combat memories and feel like you failed your Battle Buddies if they were seriously injured or killed or you may feel grief if your Buddy was killed.
Non-Defensive/Combat Driving You had to drive fast and unpredictably, using rapid lane changes and keeping other vehicles at a distance to avoid IEDs. You were used to people getting out of your way.	**Aggressive Driving** You may be easily angered while you are driving in traffic and may be inclined to drive fast. You may feel angry at drivers for no reason. You may tend to ignore traffic laws and to drive aggressively.
Discipline & Ordering Your survival depended on discipline and obeying orders. Following orders protected you and those around you and kept you safe and in control.	**Conflict** You may try to order your family and friends around, which will cause conflicts and arguments. You may find that you and your loved ones are in a constant power struggle.

M I N D

SLEEP STRUGGLES:
HOW BEING DOWNRANGE AFFECTS SLEEP

It's a fact. Soldiers in combat zones sometimes have to function with very little sleep. When you were deployed, you had to be alert and ready to respond at all times, so you could never let your guard down. The roar of aircraft and combat in the distance, incoming mortar rounds, and fellow Soldiers putting on or taking off their weapons, opening and closing doors, or shouting over video games all made it difficult to sleep. If your location and duty were downrange, you may have seen disturbing things that you couldn't get out of your mind.

But somehow, in spite of the noise, the danger, and the demands for constant vigilance, you got used to the chaos and started to feel "at home." Though you may not have been able to get a really good night's sleep, you learned how to survive on whatever sleep you could get.

Now that you've returned from your deployment, everything may seem too quiet. You may have bad memories that you think of when you try to go to sleep or that return as nightmares. You may be feeling edgy and irritable a lot of the time, which makes it difficult to settle down before you go to sleep. You can see how easy it could be to develop a sleep problem.

When we talk about sleep disturbances, we're talking about having trouble falling asleep, waking up during the night, having trouble going back to sleep, or waking up too early in the morning. When your sleep is disturbed, you often feel tired when you wake up and experience daytime sleepiness, poor concentration, and heightened irritability, which create problems in your family and social life. Sleep problems also affect your performance by causing you to make mistakes. Getting good sleep is important for you to make a smooth transition from the combat zone to home.

Are you having any problems sleeping? If so, what kinds of problems?

SNOOZE NEWS:

Here are several important tips that will help you get a good night's sleep:

Organize Your Day to Maximize Your Sleep

 Wake up and go to bed at the same time every day, even on weekends. Your body gets used to having a routine.

 Avoid consuming caffeine 4 to 6 hours before bedtime. This includes coffee, tea, sodas, and chocolate. Caffeine is a stimulant which keeps most people awake.

 Avoid drinking alcohol 4 to 6 hours before bedtime. Many people believe that alcohol helps them sleep. Although alcohol can make you drowsy so you go to sleep, when the alcohol level in your blood starts to fall, it may cause you to wake up and feel jittery.

 Limit your use of tobacco products, especially before bedtime. Nicotine is a stimulant and will keep you awake. Some people make the mistake of smoking when they wake up during the night. Nighttime smoking will keep you from going to sleep or being able to go back to sleep if you wake up.

 Avoid big meals, especially those with heavy, sugary, or spicy foods, and be sure to finish eating at least 4 to 6 hours before bedtime. Heavy foods can affect your ability to stay asleep.

Exercise regularly but don't exercise for several hours before bedtime.

Don't take naps. Falling asleep in a chair or on the couch in the afternoon or early evening is sure to cause sleep problems. If you do nap, limit it to 20 to 30 minutes.

Create the Best Possible Sleep Environment

Make sure you have a comfortable mattress and pillows. Uncomfortable bedding can interfere with your sleep.

Remove electronics like TVs and computers from your bedroom. Watching TV before bedtime is usually a bad idea. The TV can be too exciting or interesting and makes it hard to quiet your mind. Working at your computer is too challenging. Anything that activates your mind makes it hard to settle down and go to sleep.

Keep your bedroom comfortable, quiet, and dark. You will find it hard to sleep if your room is too hot or too cold. Noise and light activate your mind and make it difficult to go to sleep.

Use your bed only for sleep and sex. Don't use your bedroom as an office, recreation room, or work room. This confuses your mind. Let your body know that the bed is associated with sleep.

Getting Ready for Bed is Also Important

- ▰ Establish a relaxing bedtime routine.
- ▰ Practice relaxation techniques before bedtime and as you fall asleep.
- ▰ Don't watch the clock.
- ▰ If you can't fall asleep within 15 or 20 minutes, get out of bed. Go to a dimly lit room and practice the relaxation techniques in Chapter 6 of this book.

Easy Relaxation Exercises for Sleep

Sleep Countdown

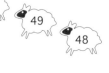

- Find a comfortable sleeping position.
- Close your eyes and take a deep breath.
- Scan your body for tension.
- Focus on relaxing tense muscles.
- Starting with the number 50, start counting backwards with each deep breath.
- Picture the numbers in your mind as you count.
- Continue to count until you reach zero.
- You will fall asleep as you count.

Fifty Heavily Carpeted Steps

- Find a comfortable sleeping position.
- Close your eyes and take a deep breath.
- Imagine you are at the top of a long flight of heavily carpeted steps.
- You are going to walk down each step slowly.
- Each time you take a breath and go down another step, you feel the soft, heavily carpeted steps under your feet.
- You keep on climbing down the steps until you reach the bottom.
- You will fall asleep before you reach the bottom of the steps.

The Blank Screen in Your Head

- Find a comfortable sleeping position.
- Close your eyes and take a deep breath.
- Roll your eyes upward and focus your attention on the middle of your forehead, as if there were a movie screen in your head.
- Every time you breathe, as you look at the screen in your head, think the word "blank." Continue to look at the screen in your head, breathe deeply, and think the word "blank"each time you breathe out. Repeat 5 times.
- Now shift your attention to any place in your body that's relaxed.
- Continue to focus your attention on the relaxed place in your body, breathe deeply, and think the word "relax" each time you breathe out. Repeat 5 times.
- Now shift your attention back to the blank screen in your head and think the word "blank" each time you breathe. Repeat 5 times.
- Now shift your attention back into the relaxed place in your body and think the word "relax." Repeat 5 times.
- Continue to shift your attention between the screen in your forehead and the relaxed place in your body, repeating the word "blank" when you focus on your forehead and the word "relax" when you focus on your body. Continue until you fall asleep.

You now understand why you may be having sleep problems and how to make the necessary changes to get a good night's sleep. You know you need to...

- Organize your day
- Create the best possible sleep environment
- Prepare for sleep

You've also learned some easy relaxation techniques to use as you go to sleep. You learned how to use...

- Sleep Countdown
- Fifty Heavily Carpeted Steps
- The Blank Screen in Your Head

What can you do to solve your sleep problems?

Now you know how to get rid of the "Snooze Blues." Good luck and enjoy your peaceful nights of sleep!

What is Stress?

We all know what it is like to feel stressed. Stress is a fact of life. It can occur as you react to the changes you must make as you adjust and respond to the demands of your continually changing world.

Do you know what makes a situation stressful for one person, while another person feels stimulated or challenged by the same set of circumstances? The answer lies in your perception, or view, of your situation. Stress occurs when you believe that the demands of the situation exceed your ability to meet those demands.

Both positive events and negative events can create stress. Most of us understand that negative events, such as the death of a loved one or financial problems, create stress. But you may not realize that positive events, such as the birth of a child, a new relationship, a job promotion, or holidays, are also stressful. As you experience stressful events, you make adjustments in your life. As you adjust to different circumstances, stress will either help or hinder you, depending on how you react to it.

Although you probably think of stress as being negative, stress can create positive or negative feelings. Stressful situations can have a positive influence on you by motivating you to take action, acquire new skills, increase your awareness, and develop a new outlook. Stress has a negative effect on you when it causes you to feel overwhelmed, rejected, angry, or depressed. Unmanaged stress can lead to health problems such as headaches, insomnia, stomach problems, rashes, high blood pressure, heart disease, and stroke.

Sources of Stress

There are different kinds of stress.

Physical stress refers to your body's physical reaction to triggers, such as the pain you experience after an injury.

Environmental stress is caused by things like weather, noise, pollution, and traffic.

Social stress includes financial problems, job demands, arguments, and the loss of someone you love.

 Emotional stress is caused by your thoughts, especially when you think the demands of a situation exceed your ability to meet the demands.

How Stress Affects You

A stress reaction occurs when you feel threatened. This reaction, known as the "fight or flight response," prepares you to deal with danger and accounts for the survival of our species. It also helps you to survive when you are in combat.

Now that you're home, you may feel like you are still in danger, even though you're not. If you don't learn how to manage your stress, you may develop serious health problems. These are some reactions you may have when you feel overwhelmed by situations you consider stressful:

- You may feel irritable, jumpy, and tense.

- You may have difficulty sleeping, which leaves you feeling tired and unable to work effectively or make good decisions.

- Your muscles may become tense, leading to headaches, backaches, clenched teeth and sore jaws, or overall muscle pain.

- You may have stomach aches, acid reflux, nausea, or diarrhea.

- Your blood pressure may increase, and your heart may race or your heartbeat may be irregular.

- You may feel dizzy and have difficulty breathing.

Simple Stress Solutions for Soldiers

In this section, I am going to help you learn some simple techniques for reducing your stress. This will give you more control when you are feeling overwhelmed by negative thoughts, feelings, or memories. These techniques are especially useful when your anger has been triggered and you are having trouble controlling your behavior.

BREATHING

Stress triggers the "arousal system" in your body so that you can respond immediately to the demands of a situation you consider threatening. Did you know that you also have a "recovery system" in your body? There is actually a special kind of breathing that triggers a part of your nervous system to calm you down.

Breathing is the one activity that is essential to life. When you inhale, you take in the oxygen your brain and body need to sustain life. When you exhale, you release carbon dioxide, which is a waste product.

Poor breathing habits deprive your brain and body of the oxygen you need to deal with stressful situations. Shallow breathing can cause you to feel anxious and stressed. The first step in changing the effects of stress on your body is to become aware of your breathing pattern. Learning to breathe correctly can help you to reduce your stress reaction.

It might help to think about your arousal and recovery systems as if they were parts of your truck. When your nervous system is geared up, it's like having your foot on the accelerator. That's fine when you need that energy to be sharp and focused, like you do when you are doing your job or you're completing a mission. But long-term activation of your arousal system causes your body to become depleted. That's why unmanaged stress leads to health problems. Learning to breathe correctly triggers your recovery system, like putting your brakes on. It brings the brain into balance and causes your body to relax.

Before I teach you this special kind of deep breathing, I'm going to help you become more aware of your breathing patterns.

BREATHING AWARENESS

1. Close your eyes.
2. Put your right hand on your abdomen right above your navel at your waistline.
3. Put your left hand on the center of your chest.
4. Without changing your breathing, notice how you are breathing. Which hand rises the most when you inhale? Is it the hand on your chest or the hand on your belly? If it's the hand on your chest, your breathing is shallow. If it's the hand on your belly, your breathing is deep. Which one do you think is better for you? If you said deep breathing, you were right. That's the kind of breathing that will help you calm down and reduce your stress.

Now I am going to guide you through a deep breathing exercise for a few minutes as you read. This will work best if you practice it in a quiet place where you won't be disturbed.

DEEP BREATHING

In the following exercise, you are going to take 5 slow deep breaths. You will breathe in as you count to 6, hold your breath for 3 counts, then breathe out as you count to 6. When you breathe in, your hand will move out. When you breathe out, your hand will move in.

1. Put your right hand on your abdomen right above your navel at your waistline.
2. Now *breathe in* slowly as you count to 6; your hand moves out.
3. Pause as you count to 3.
4. Now *breathe out* as you count to 6; your hand moves in.
5. Now *breathe in* as you count to 6; your hand moves out.
6. Pause as you count to 3.
7. Now *breathe out* as you count to 6; your hand moves in.
8. Now *breathe in* as you count to 6; your hand moves out.
9. Pause as you count to 3.
10. Now *breathe out* as you count to 6; your hand moves in.
11. Now *breathe in* as you count to 6; your hand moves out.
12. Pause as you count to 3.
13. Now *breathe out* as you count to 6; your hand moves in.
14. Now *breathe in* as you count to 6; your hand moves out.
15. Pause as you count to 3.
16. Now *breathe out* as you count to 6; your hand moves in.

You may notice that just a few breaths have left you feeling more relaxed. You are already beginning to learn how to trigger your recovery system to calm you down.

You may practice this lying down. Lie on your back in a comfortable position with one hand on your belly again in front of your belly button. When you breathe in, your hand will rise. As you breathe out, your hand will fall. If you still have trouble knowing if you are breathing correctly, you can put a book on your abdomen. The book rises as you breathe in. The book comes back down as you breathe out.

TENSION RELEASE

1. Sit comfortably in your chair with your feet flat on the floor.
2. Take a deep breath into your belly while you say to yourself, "I'm breathing in relaxation." Put your left hand on the center of your chest.
3. Pause for a moment before you exhale.
4. Breathe out all the air from your abdomen while you say to yourself, "I'm breathing out the tension."
5. Each time you breathe in, notice if there is any tension in your body.
6. Each time you breathe out, let go of any bodily tension you have noticed.
7. You may find it helpful to think of breathing in plus signs (+), which stand for positive, and to think of breathing out minus signs (-), which stand for negative.

BODY AWARENESS

Body awareness exercises help you become more aware of your bodily reactions to stress. You will feel less stressed when you learn to become aware of your tension and release it.

BODY SCANNING

1. Close your eyes.
2. Putting your attention on your toes and moving up through your body, find the parts of your body that are tense. Ask yourself, "Where am I tense?"
3. When you find a tense area, tense those muscles even more.
4. Notice that you are creating the tension in your body.
5. Then take a deep breath and relax the muscles while you say to yourself the word "Relax."
6. Try to figure out what life situation may be causing tensions in your body.
7. Now try to figure out what you can do to change the situation causing your tension.

EXTERNAL VS. INTERNAL AWARENESS

1. Focus your attention on the outside world. Notice what's going on around you and say to yourself "I am aware of…" For example, "I am aware of the conversation my Buddies are having." "I am aware of the brightness of the sun." "I am aware of the smell of food coming from the mess hall."
2. After you have become aware of everything going on around you, shift your attention to the physical sensations of your body. For example, "I am aware of feeling hungry." "I am aware of tension in my lower back."
3. Switch back and forth between being aware of things going on in the outside world and things going on inside.
4. This exercise helps you to be aware of the difference between your inner and outer worlds, which can help you separate yourself from things in the outside world that irritate you.

MUSCLE RELAXATION

Like most people, you probably don't realize that your muscles are tense until they start to hurt, as they do when you have a headache or a backache. Muscle relaxation training can help you recognize when your muscles are tense.

You are going to tense each muscle group for 5 seconds and relax for 20 seconds. Notice the difference between tension and relaxation each time you tense and relax the muscles.

1. Curl both fists and tighten your biceps and forearms (strongman pose). Hold for 5 seconds. Notice the tension.
2. Now relax your fists, biceps and forearms for 20 seconds. Notice the relaxation in the muscles.
3. Now roll your head around on your neck in a complete circle. Then roll your head around the other direction.
4. Now relax your head.
5. Now tense all the muscles of your face by wrinkling your forehead, squinting your eyes, opening your mouth, and hunching your shoulders. Hold for 5 seconds. Notice the tension.
6. Now relax for 20 seconds. Notice the difference between the tension and relaxation.
7. Now take a deep breath into your chest as you arch your shoulders back. Hold the position for 5 seconds. Notice the tension.
8. Now relax for 20 seconds.
9. Now take a deep breath while you push out your stomach. Hold for 5 seconds. Notice the tension.
10. Now relax for 20 seconds.
11. Now straighten your legs and point your toes back toward your face. Hold for 5 seconds. Notice the tension.
12. Now relax for 20 seconds.
13. Now straighten your legs and curl your toes as you tighten your calves, thighs, and buttocks. Hold for 5 seconds. Notice the tension.
14. Now relax for 20 seconds. You will notice that all the muscles in your body are more relaxed than they were before you did this exercise.

You now understand how stress is affecting you and how to make the necessary changes to reduce your stress. You know you need to:

- identify your sources of stress

- recognize how stress is affecting you

- use stress management techniques

What techniques can you use to reduce your stress?

RAGE GAUGE

What is Anger?

Anger is an intense emotion which you usually experience in response to opposition, mistreatment, injury, or a feeling of helplessness. It is an unpleasant and uncomfortable feeling — part of the "fight or flight response" — which is there to protect you by making you want to fight back against whatever is causing the feeling.

You don't have to feel angry to be a Soldier or to fight in combat. However, war zone situations like working in extreme conditions, having to use broken equipment, and facing sniper fire can cause a constant state of frustration. It doesn't help when you hear about problems at home. The angry feelings become so familiar that they become second nature. The anger can even begin to feel like it's a part of who you are.

Most Soldiers say that the most common problem they have when they return from a deployment is feeling angry a lot of the time. Do you agree? Think for a moment about the things you think about that make you feel angry.

Here's a list of common anger triggers, also known as "hot buttons," among Soldiers after they return from a deployment:

Traffic. Most Soldiers say that they feel frustrated and often feel angry when they are driving. You are probably used to traveling in a Humvee. When you were deployed, you could drive fast and people would get out of your way. Now that you're home, driving in traffic is frustrating. You have to drive more slowly than you are used to, and it seems like other people are driving too slowly. You want to get where you are going fast, just like you did when you were in the combat zone.

Civilians. A lot of Soldiers say that civilians' behavior gets on their nerves when they are out in public, especially when they hear a civilian complaining about things that aren't important. You may think that civilians have no idea of what you have been through. You may think that civilians have it easy and have no appreciation for the freedom you risked your life for in the combat zone.

Family members. Most Soldiers are really happy to be home with family. But it doesn't take long before you begin to feel angry at all the demands your family is putting on you. You may feel like your family wants you to spend too much time with them. You may think they expect too much of you. You may get really irritated when they move your stuff around and don't do what you want or tell them to do. You may find out that they didn't take care of things while you were gone, that they spent too much money, or that they made bad choices that you have to deal with now that you're home.

Your spouse or partner. A lot of Soldiers feel really irritated when their spouse or partner starts asking about their deployment experiences. You may feel uncomfortable when they show emotions like sadness or fear. You may wish they could control their emotions like you do.

Other military personnel. You may find yourself angry with other Soldiers who have easier jobs. Maybe they have medical or emotional problems that made them undeployable. Maybe they are in units that don't deploy to combat zones. Maybe they have jobs that aren't as dangerous as yours. Maybe they're at posts that received equipment and weapons you needed but didn't have.

Politicians. You may feel angry at politicians and government officials. You may think they don't understand how hard your job is. You may think they don't know how hard it is for you to be away from your family during deployments to hostile lands or what a negative effect the deployments are having on you. You may feel angry because you think they don't really care. You may feel like a statistic—just a number, not a person with feelings and loved ones who are suffering the effects of your absence during your deployment.

There are many other things which may make you feel angry. Some may seem like small or insignificant things that don't seem to matter to anyone else.

What are some of your Hot Buttons?

YOUR ANGER TANK

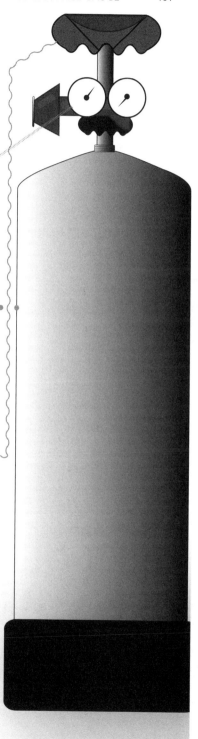

One way to think about your anger is to think of yourself as having an Anger Tank. Let's look closely at the parts of a gas cylinder and how it works. What are the most important parts of the tank?

There is the *cylinder* where the gas is stored.

There are *gauges* that indicate how much gas is in the cylinder, how much pressure is being exerted, and the temperature of the cylinder.

There is a *release valve* on the top of the cylinder.

Because the contents of a gas cylinder are under pressure and sometimes hazardous, there are special safety regulations for handling it. Under heat, the pressure of a gas cylinder rises in direct proportion to its temperature. If the internal pressure gets too high and there are no means to safely vent the pressurized gas, the cylinder will explode.

Causes of Anger

In order to keep your Anger Tank from exploding, you need to understand what causes anger.

- *Trigger.* First, there is an event which serves as a trigger.

- *Thoughts.* Next, when something negative happens, you start thinking. If the event seems dangerous, your thoughts alert you to the need to get away fast. If you interpret the event as something offensive, wrong, unfair, deliberate, or preventable that causes difficulty, pain, or distress to you or someone you care about, you probably think that punishment is justified. The "hot" angry thoughts cause the anger in your tank to build.

- *Physical arousal.* When an event triggers negative thoughts, your body goes into "fight or flight" mode. If the event seems dangerous, you go into "flight" mode to get away from danger. If the event seems offensive, you go into "fight" mode and prepare to deliver punishment. Either way, your body gets geared up for action.

- *Behavior.* When an event triggers angry thoughts and the desire to fight, you may find yourself in a tough spot. Your training as a Soldier has taught you to respond to danger automatically with targeted aggression. Back at home, your anger can be very destructive to your relationships and, in the long run, to your physical health.

Pressure in Your Anger Tank

Your behavior may become hazardous to you and others when the pressure and heat increase in your anger tank. The demands that are put on you when you return from a deployment can cause the pressure in your anger tank to build. The **"HOT" ANGRY THOUGHTS** you have about those demands may cause the pressure to build until you feel like you are going to explode.

What happens when your Anger Tank is under too much pressure or gets too hot? It will explode if there is no way to release the built-up pressure. If you don't recognize that the pressure is building or know how to release that pressure and turn down the heat, your anger may explode into rage and violence.

Here are some common triggers that may cause the pressure in your Anger Tank to build:

- Expectations of family and friends that you spend time with them when you want to be alone or with your Battle Buddies.

- Being in large groups or around civilians.

- Driving in traffic.

- Being without your weapon.

- Being asked about your deployment experiences.

- Seeing your spouse or girlfriend cry.

What are some of the causes of your anger that increase the pressure in your Anger Tank?

Your Rage Gauge

A pressure gauge is an instrument designed to measure pressure. Every gas cylinder has one to make sure the pressure in the cylinder is not too high. A temperature gauge indicates whether the temperature is too high. Your **Rage Gauge** is going to tell you how much pressure and heat are in your Anger Tank. To prevent the pressure in your Anger Tank from becoming too high, you need to become familiar with your **Rage Gauge.**

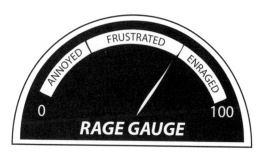

There are several things you can do to get to know your **Rage Gauge:**

- *Monitor your bodily reactions.* Is your heart beating faster? Do you feel shaky? Is your hand curled up in a fist? Are your muscles tense? Are you starting to feel hot and sweaty?

- *Notice your triggers and hot buttons.* Are there certain things that push your buttons and make you go from 0 to 100 in a split second?

- *Think about your expectations.* Do you have unrealistic expectations of yourself or others?

- *Check out your thoughts and assumptions.* Are you exaggerating the importance of what has happened? Are you fanning old coals of resentment? Are you remembering past hurts you've been carrying around as you deal with what is going on now?

Imagine that your Rage Gauge goes from 1 to 100. A lower reading, like 10 or 20, represents annoyance or irritation. A medium reading, 30 or 40, indicates frustration and building pressure. When the reading gets over 50, you need to start paying attention. Your Rage Gauge is telling you that the pressure and heat are building and that you may be headed for an explosion.

I'm sure you know that the pressure in your Anger Tank can cause you to have physical problems like headaches, stomach aches, and high blood pressure, and emotional problems like anxiety and depression. High blood pressure can be a real problem because medication for hypertension can cause you to have problems in your sex life. Antidepressants also have negative sexual side effects.

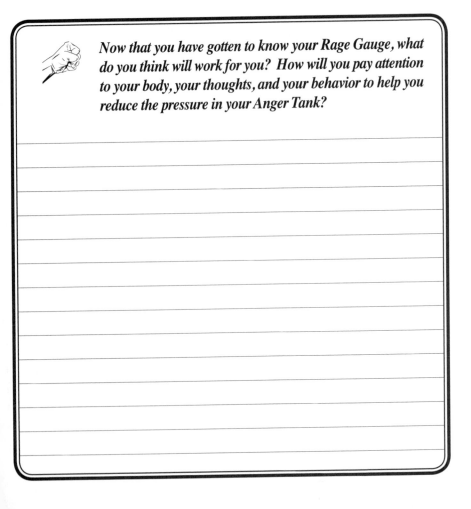

Now that you have gotten to know your Rage Gauge, what do you think will work for you? How will you pay attention to your body, your thoughts, and your behavior to help you reduce the pressure in your Anger Tank?

Your Release Valves

A cylinder has a release valve to control or limit pressure which can build up and cause equipment failure, fire, or an explosion. When you know how to make good use of your angry energy, it will help you manage the pressure in your Anger Tank.

Are you wondering what I mean by "good use of your angry energy"? You may think that your anger is bad because it has been destructive to you and your relationships in the past. But remember, anger is an energy state that is designed to solve problems and to protect you. You can learn to use the energy in ways that aren't destructive and to release the excess energy.

Here are some positive ways to release your angry energy:

- Run, jog, or take a vigorous walk.
- Exercise vigorously for 15 to 30 minutes.
- Work outside in the yard.
- Talk with your Buddy or spouse about your anger.
- Write about your angry feelings. When you're done, you may want to put the paper through a shredder or delete the file if you used your computer.

What release valves will work best for you to prevent the build-up of angry energy?

Rethinking Your Anger

You have learned how important your thoughts are in managing your anger. Here are some examples of anger-arousing thoughts that increase the pressure in your Anger Tank and can result in angry behavior:

- Blaming: "It's your fault, not mine!"

- Injustice: "That's not fair! You're not treating me right! I deserve better than this!"

- Rigid thinking: "You need to do it my way! It's the way things should be done!"

- Extreme thinking: "Those people are so stupid! What's the matter with them?!"

- Awfulizing: "I can't stand this for another minute! I've got to get out of here!"

Here are some examples of anger-reducing thoughts that can decrease the pressure in your Anger Tank and keep you from saying or doing something you may regret:

- "Sometimes bad things happen. It's nobody's fault."

- "Everybody makes mistakes. They couldn't help it."

- "I'm not going to waste my energy and get angry about this. It's really not that important."

- "People are not always going to do things the way I want them done. It's not realistic to expect that."

- "No matter how angry I get, I can't really control how other people act. I'd better work on controlling my own actions rather than trying to control everyone else."

What are some of the triggers and "hot" angry thoughts you have that increase the pressure in your anger tank? How can you rethink your anger?

Anger Habits

You may not realize it, but you may have developed some Anger Habits. Here are some habits that intensify your anger:

- Accusations: "You never do anything right!"
- Inflammatory statements: "If you don't do what I say, you'll live to regret it!"
- Personal attacks: "You're an idiot! I don't know what's wrong with you!"
- Yelling
- Arguing
- Plotting Revenge
- Violence
- Pouting and Sulking

You may need to develop some habits that help you cool off, like the ones listed below:

- Notice what you're thinking and saying.
- Use "I statements" instead of accusatory "you statements." Instead of saying "You make me so angry," say "I feel angry when you do that."
- Count to ten.
- Take a time out.
- Think before you speak.
- Realize that the other person has power over you when you're angry at them and and learn to let things go.
- Be a duck, not a sponge. Let things roll off your back like water off a duck's back instead of absorbing them like a sponge and letting them sour.
- Exercise.
- Use the Three-Minute Rule. If you haven't begun to resolve a conflict in three minutes, things are only going to get worse. You're better off to take a breather and calm down rather than to continue to argue.

What anger habits have you developed? What can you do to change them?

ALCOHOL ALERT

During your deployment, you weren't able to drink much, if any, alcohol. Once you return home, there are a lot of opportunities to drink.

Drinking after deployment can be tricky. Most Soldiers want to celebrate their return with their friends and family. Alcohol is often a part of the social scene. It's cheap, readily available, and socially acceptable. It's sometimes hard to know when you have crossed the line from social drinking to binge drinking.

Your alcohol tolerance decreased while you were deployed, so you will need to go slowly to relearn your limit. You might have been able to handle 5 or 6 drinks before you left. Now 3 or 4 drinks may have the same effect. It may take a lot less alcohol to slow down your coordination and judgment.

Some Soldiers drink when they have too much time on their hands. It can be easy to start drinking when you are alone and feeling bored. You will need to be careful of excessive use, especially if you drink often.

WATCH OUT! DON'T GET RISKY WITH WHISKEY OR INTO A DRUNK FUNK!

Here are some ways alcohol can cause problems:

Avoiding or Masking Feelings

● You may not realize that you are using alcohol as a release valve for uncomfortable emotions. Drinking alcohol may seem to provide some relief at first, but over time, it can cause a lot of problems for you and your relationships.

● Soldiers sometimes use alcohol to reduce their anxiety about returning home and reestablishing relationships. Some Soldiers use alcohol to "numb out" when they feel anxious. Other Soldiers feel numb most of the time and consume alcohol so they can feel again. After a couple of drinks, they begin to feel good. To keep the good feeling, they "chase the high" by consuming more alcohol. Continuing to drink to keep feeling good can push your blood alcohol to high levels of intoxication, which can cause you to get drunk and engage in risky behavior that you don't remember or to pass out.

● Alcohol can be used to avoid dealing with bad memories, trauma issues, and survivor guilt.

● Heavy alcohol use can trigger sadness, depression, anxiety, and anger.

Creating Relationship Problems

● Alcohol abuse can interfere with your relationships by reducing emotional closeness.

● Alcohol can impair parenting skills.

Interfering with Sleep

○ Drinking alcohol can interfere with your sleep. Because alcohol can make you feel tired, you may drink to help you go to sleep. But if you drink within an hour of bedtime, you may wake up feeling jittery during the second half of your sleep cycle and have trouble going back to sleep.

○ Over time, if you keep drinking before bedtime, alcohol's sleep-inducing effect may decrease, and its disruptive effects may increase.

○ Heavy alcohol use can trigger nightmares.

Causing Serious Health Problems

○ Heavy alcohol use can lead to cardiovascular and liver disease.

○ Alcohol in combination with prescription or over the counter (OTC) drugs can cause serious health problems.

Being a Career Buster

○ Alcohol abuse can ruin your career by increasing the likelihood of violence, arrest, DUIs, etc.

Here are some questions to ask yourself about your alcohol use:

How is easy access to alcohol affecting you now that you are home? Do you find yourself drinking more than you used to?

Do you and your buddies tend to go out drinking together?

Do you use alcohol to calm down, get to sleep, chill out, or numb your feelings?

Has alcohol interfered with your relationships at home?

Has anyone told you that they are concerned about your drinking?

Have you gotten into any legal trouble since you returned home?

How are your post-deployment drinking habits different from your patterns before you deployed?

146 AT EASE, SOLDIER!

Do you think that alcohol is affecting your mood, your relationships with your family or friends, or your job performance? If so, how?

Be careful not to use alcohol to calm down, when you are feeling depressed, or to numb your feelings. And don't drink if you are having trouble sleeping. Alcohol will cause sleep problems by interfering with the stages of sleep and preventing you from getting the sound, restorative rest you need.

Remember to H.A.L.T. Times to be extra careful with your alcohol use are when you're Hungry (H), Angry (A), Lonely (L), or Tired (T).

CONCLUSION

While you were deployed, things happened around you and to you that have changed who you are. In this book, I have provided information that has helped you understand how your training and deployment experiences have changed you.

You have learned how to leave the war downrange so that you don't have a war raging in your mind. You have learned how to recognize when you're stressed out and how that affects you. You have developed some skills that are helping you to sleep better, control the jitters, manage your anger, and adjust to your life at home.

Here are a few of the important things you learned from this book:

★ During deployment to combat zones, Soldiers experience events which change the way they see themselves, their relationships to others, and their place in the world.

★ Being in a combat zone has an impact on every Soldier mentally and emotionally. All Soldiers are different when they return from deployment.

★ During your training, you learned important survival skills that have made you a good Soldier. It is crucial that you not let the survival skills you learned and your combat behaviors and reactions determine how you respond at home.

★ You have become a part of a new family, your Battle Buddies. At home, you may feel that others, even your family and friends, don't understand what you have been through. You may feel that you don't fit in and it may be difficult for you to feel "at home."

Here are more of the important things you learned in this book:

★ Your family needs to know about your deployment experiences so they can understand you better.

★ At home, numbing out, detaching, and failing to express your emotions or only showing anger is harmful to your relationships. Expressing your emotions appropriately to your spouse and to your friends is an important part of keeping your personal relationships healthy.

★ Your family members have been in charge of making decisions while you were deployed and will want to continue to make decisions for themselves.

★ Your family and friends are not members of your military unit. You will need to be prepared to negotiate.

★ At home, you may continue to feel keyed up or revved up all the time, especially when you are in large groups or situations where you feel confined.

★ When you return home, you may feel the need to continue to be armed. You will have to think of other ways to feel safe.

★ It is important for you to learn to control your anger. You will need to learn to walk away when you feel angry and to shift from offensive to defensive driving.

★ Learning to manage your stress will be important to your physical and emotional health. If you don't know how to manage your stress, you may develop health problems, anxiety, or depression.

★ Learning to breathe correctly triggers your recovery system. It brings the brain into balance and causes your body to relax.

★ Drinking alcohol before bedtime can interfere with your sleep.

★ Heavy alcohol use can trigger sadness, nightmares, depression, and anger and can cause problems in your relationships.

You now have the tools you need to help you leave your deployment experiences in the past where they belong and adjust to your present life at home. Reading this book, learning and practicing the techniques, and completing the exercises has already helped you begin to feel at home and to create the life you want.

Being exposed to life-threatening situations can leave you anxious and confused, but it can also help you to recognize what is important in your life. Feeling at home in your own skin, knowing how to enjoy being with those who love you, being able to share your deepest fears and disappointments without fear of judgment or rejection, being free of terrible memories that haunt you — these are all things you know you want. I encourage you to continue to think about the life you want and to use what you have learned to create the satisfying life you deserve.

Good luck!

Please record your completion date. You deserve a Medal of Valor for the courage it has taken to complete the exercises in this book.

CONGRATULATIONS!
Completion Date:
/   /

Here's some extra writing space, in case you have anything else to unload from your truck...

ACKNOWLEDGMENTS

First and foremost, I would like to thank all the courageous Soldiers who have sacrificed their safety and the comforts of home to preserve my fredom and the freedom of my family. I would also like to thank their families for the sacrifices they made as they endured the hardship of managing the home front while their Soldiers were deployed.

To all of the Soldiers, veterans, and military spouses who reviewed the materials in this book: thank you for your comments, suggestions, and feedback, which were an essential part of the book's creation. This book would never have been written without your assistance, encouragement, interest, and enthusiasm. Special thanks go to Kristen Elpel, a member of my staff, whose husband was deployed to Iraq during the book's creation and whose suggestions were especially helpful.

Thanks to Stacey Graham, Practice Manager, who managed my schedule so that I could balance my work seeing patients at my office while also writing the manuscript for the book.

Special thanks to Maryellen Courter, who provided the graphic design and cover art for this book. Thank you for working steadfastly on the project to create this very unique book designed to help Soldiers in their adjustment from the war zone to home. Thank you for doing the necessary research and for using your ingenuity to create images with special meaning for the Soldiers and their families. And thank you for working tirelessly to "get it right" and being so open to feedback.

I would like to thank Bettie Sogor, Ph.D., a worthy mentor, trusted friend, and respected colleague. Thank you, Bettie, for your tireless effort on my behalf, your dedication and commitment to the creation of this book, and your encouragement and vision for future projects.

I would also like to thank Connie Edwards, Business Consultant, and Lynn Vos, Area Director, for the Georgia Small Business Development Center Network in Savannah. Thank you, Connie and Lynn, for recognizing the importance of this project and extending your encouragement, support, and expertise. You have made a tremendous difference!

Last, but certainly not least, I would like to thank my family for their continued belief and support as I worked on the manuscript. To my parents, Louise and William Stubbs, thank you for teaching me the importance of determination and persistence. To my husband, Barry, thank you for your understanding, endurance, encouragement and unwavering belief in me and my projects over the years. To my children, Pat, Webb, Greg, Ben, and John Paul: thank you for your inspiration, creativity, and commitment to be of service to humankind. To their spouses and children, thank you for providing balance and hope for the future. Special thanks to Pat, John Paul, and Jannie for the countless hours you spent reviewing the manuscript and providing feedback.

About the Author

Dr. Gayle Rozantine is a clinical psychologist specializing in stress management, post traumatic stress disorder (PTSD), and health psychology. She earned two master's degrees, one in education from Emory University, and the other in clinical psychology from Western Carolina University. She was awarded her doctorate in clinical psychology from the University of Tennessee and completed an internship and a fellowship in Behavioral Medicine from the Georgia Health Sciences University.

During her clinical training, Dr. Rozantine worked extensively with veterans of the Vietnam War, including veterans receiving inpatient treatment for PTSD. She is currently in private practice in Savannah, Georgia, and provides treatment for Soldiers stationed at Ft. Stewart and Hunter Army Air Field and their families.

Dr. Rozantine is a Diplomate and is Board Certified in Stress Management by the American Academy of Experts in Traumatic Stress and is a member of the National Center for Crisis Management, the National Register of Health Care Providers in Psychology, the American Psychological Association, and the Georgia Psychological Association.

Dr. Rozantine has written numerous articles and developed a wellness series for use in corporate wellness programs. She has recorded CDs that teach relaxation training and assist in improving self esteem.

Website: www.SoldiersAtHome.com

REFERENCE
AND READING LIST

Armstrong, Keith, Best, Suzanne, Domenici, Paula (2006). *Courage after Fire*. Berkeley, CA.: Ulysses Press.

Battlemind Training 1: Transitioning from Combat to Home. Walter Reed Army Institute of Research (WRAIR), U.S. Army Medical Research and Material Command. http://www.behavioralhealth.army.mil/battlemind/WRAIR_Battlemind_Training_I_Brochure_Final.pdf.

Battlemind Training 2: Continuing the Transition Home. Walter Reed Army Institute of Research (WRAIR), U.S. Army Medical Research and Material Command. http://www.behavioralhealth.army.mil/battlemind/BattlemindTrainingII.pdf.

Benson, Herbert (1975). *The Relaxation Response*. NY: Harper Collins.

Cantrell, Bridget C., Dean, Chuck (2005). *Down Range to Iraq and Back*. Seattle, WA: WordSmith Publishing.

Davis, Martha, Eschelman, Elizabeth, McKay, Matthew, Fanning, Patrick (2008). *The Relaxation and Stress Reduction Workbook,* Oakland, CA: New Harbinger Publications, Inc.

Dual Recovery Anonymous World Network Central. http://www.draonline.org/relapse5.html

e-Health MD: *Stress and How to Manage It: What is Stress?* http://www.ehealthmd.com/library/stress/STR_whatis.html

Jacobs, Gregg (1998). *Say Goodnight to Insomnia: A Drug-Free Program Developed at Harvard Medical School*. NY: Henry Hold & Company.

Kassinove, Howard, Tafrate, Raymond (2002). *Anger Management: The Complete Treatment Guidebook for Practitioners*. Atascadero, CA: Impact Publishers, Inc.

Kuhn, Cynthia, Swartzwelder, Scott, Wilson, Wilkie (2008). *Buzzed: The Straight Facts About the Most Used and Abused Drugs from Alcohol to Ecstasy* (Third Edition).NY: W/W. Norton & Company, Inc.

London, Robert (2004). *Helping Patients Conquer Insomnia*. www.eclinicalpsychiatrynew.com.

PRODUCT LIST & DESCRIPTION

For online information about ordering *At Ease, Soldier!*,
as well as a variety of relaxation CDs please visit:
www.SoldiersAtHome.com

BOOKS:

At Ease, Soldier!

At Ease, Soldier! teaches you how to leave the war downrange, so that your relationships don't turn into a battlefield. This book helps you understand how your training and deployment experiences have affected you and gives you the tools you need to make the transition from the war zone to home.

RELAXATION CDS:

To help you learn how to manage your stress more effectively, Dr. Rozantine has created a collection of CDs which combine the tranquil sounds of nature and relaxation training. Listening to these CDs will teach you a skill that will help you cope with the stresses of everyday life in an entirely different way.

Relaxation Training By The Sea CD
In *Relaxation Training By The Sea,* you will learn to relax while listening to the tranquil sounds of waves as they roll onto the beach and out into the vastness of the ocean, washing away feelings of tension and stress.

Relaxation Training On A Rainy Day CD
In *Relaxation Training On A Rainy Day*, you will learn to relax while you enjoy being in a mountain cabin during a rainstorm. You will come away from this peaceful experience feeling calm and refreshed.

Relaxation Training By The Mountain Stream CD
In *Relaxation Training By The Mountain Stream*, you will learn to relax while you sit on a large rock next to a mountain stream. You will enjoy the sounds of rippling water as it flows over the rock and pebbles of the mountain stream, carrying away your worries and concerns.

Relaxation Training At A Mountain Lodge CD
In *Relaxation Training At A Mountain Lodge,* you will learn how to unwind while you take a relaxing trip to a mountain lodge. You will enjoy sitting in a comfortable leather chair in front of a large river-rock fireplace, watching the sunset and feeling the warmth of the fire. You will feel calm and peaceful as you let your worries drift away with the smoke as it swirls above the roaring fire.

ORDER FORM

For online information about ordering *At Ease, Soldier!*,
as well as a variety of relaxation CDs please visit:
www.SoldiersAtHome.com

For Mail Orders:
400 Commercial Court
Savannah, GA 31406

For Fax Orders:
912.352.9506.
Send this form.

Book or CD Title	Price	Quantity	Total
At Ease, Soldier!	$19.95		
Relaxation Training By The Sea CD	$15.95		
Relaxation Training at a Mountain Lodge CD	$15.95		
Relaxation Training by the Mountain Stream CD	$15.95		
Relaxation Training on a Rainy Day CD	$15.95		
Shipping & Handling for the book/CDs	$4.00 each		
7% tax for GA residents			
GRAND TOTAL			

Name: _____

Address: _____

City: _____ State: _____ Zip: _____

Signature: _____

Credit Card: (circle one)   Visa   Mastercard

Credit Card number: _____

Expiration: _____ Security Code: _____